George Henry Martin

A Song for My Son

George Henry Martin

A Song for My Son

ISBN/EAN: 9783744769150

Printed in Europe, USA, Canada, Australia, Japan

Cover: Foto ©ninafisch / pixelio.de

More available books at **www.hansebooks.com**

A SONG FOR MY SON.

BY

GEORGE HENRY MARTIN.

" Veritas temporis filia."

LONDON:

WATTS & CO., 17, JOHNSON'S COURT, FLEET STREET.

1890.

This from the humblest in the ranks
Of Thought rebellious ; and content
The bowman if his sheaf be spent
Only in harassing the flanks
Of prideful Wrong's great armament.

Though Pain must aye of Life be part,
Nor while the world shall spin its round
May Sin be slain or Evil bound—
By league of hand and brain and heart,
At least, may Falsehood be discrowned.

PROEM.

A MIGHTY monarch lived of old, an empire wide and fair was his ;
Unfathomable oceans rolled 'tween realm and realm—far provinces
Whose kinglets were his vassals true, by him alone upheld in place,
And, rendering their homage due, existing only by his grace.
By wondrous kingly craft he bound these units in one system vast,
That so his watchful eye was round the whole of his dominion cast.

His single will did hold in check these realms diverse, nigh numberless ;
Each prince thereof obeyed his beck.   Potent to punish or redress,
Avenge all crime, and right all wrong ; to slay or save, to crush or raise,
Howe'er remote, high-placed, or strong, howe'er concealed in hidden ways
The evil-doers or the good, so wise and powerful was he : thus,
His kingship was a fatherhood, just, merciful, ubiquitous.

Though, pity 'tis, for us are lost the precious archives of his reign,
Beneath the mould of many a host, on long-forgotten battle-plain,
'Neath cities buried in the sands, lay certain tablets graven o'er ;
These came to light, in many lands ; thereby we know that, long before
Recorded epochs of our race, there did exist such realm as his,
Though now the curious cannot trace that ancient kingdom's boundaries.

This monarch, with some deep intent, but unrevealed (nor scroll nor
  stone
Is left for our enlightenment, so this must needs remain unknown),
Conceived a method passing strange to practise with a certain isle—
One small, but fair, and within range of his own trumpets—for a while.
He suddenly, not deigning word of change in purpose to the few
There dwelling (a barbaric herd), all signs of sovereignty withdrew !

His court, his ministers, his seat of judgment, and his glittering guard
Were straight removed afar; complete was the abandonment; nor ward,
Nor aid, nor countenance of him had that lone people any more.
Savage they were, yet weak, and dim of intellect, and harassed sore
On every side by ruthless foes: where should they look for help—to
  whom ?
Royal force withdrawn, great were their woes, and miserable seemed
  their doom.

This king had ever sought to train his people to rely in chief
On their own strength and skill ; in vain their supplications for relief
Ere they had strenuously wrought their utmost—all that in them lay,
Of craft or talent leaving naught untried, and in th' incessant fray
Acquitting them as valiant men, well plying hand or wielding blade ;
Then—for he knew—and not till then, did he put forth his hand to aid.

What, then, had moved their father-king to leave them in such plight as
  this ?
Not wrath at some great trespassing, for sure such method were not his;
His anger raged not, blind, to smite alike the greater and the less,
Making his enemies to bite the dust in mere vindictiveness
(Like one whereof we read); his laws were plain, their penalties direct ;
His proclamation ran : " Such cause, inevitable such effect."

Propitiation had no part—no power—availed not a whit ;
Nay, all untutored in such art, this simple race knew naught of it.
Neither vicarious sacrifice ; one, sure, had been accounted mad

To name such thing, and in their eyes iniquitous the judge that bade
The culprit go unpunished, free, because a guiltless substitute
Stood ready 'neath the gallows-tree ; such freak had struck them wonder-
  mute.

They looked to reap as they had sown, nor other outcome held they
  meet ;
For thus their king had taught, and shown how that the fruitage, rank
  or sweet,
Would follow, poisoning or to bless, as surely as the day to night.
For law to lack that steadfastness these folk had deemed a piteous
  plight.
(Though seeming stern, methinks that mode were in the end more mer-
  ciful,
And more king-worthy than a code caprice or wrath may render null.)

Thus much these island-dwellers knew, and 'twas sufficient for their needs.
Small knowledge ; yea, but known for *true*, of greater worth than all
  our creeds.
And this each did apply within the round of his necessities.
What arts he had were naught akin to ours : small craft was his
To build, and little skill of hand to work in wood and stone ; for aught
Of this, if needed in the land, the king's deft-handed agents wrought.

And for the rest ; to guard his den, where lay his love and little ones,
From hungry beast or hostile men, and so to train his agile sons ;
To risk his life to find them food, or lose it shielding them from harm ;
The mother so to rear her brood that, fleet of foot and strong of arm,
Quick of resource and sharp of eye, subtle of wit and brave of heart,
They held their own, nor feared to die—sufficĕd *this*, they'd done
  their part.

So were they left.   But since on none, before, was condemnation passed
But always the transgressing one well knew how came he to be cast
For death or durance, this, their doom—to be abandoned by their
  king—

Seemed the more cruel from one of whom they ne'er had dreamed so
    hard a thing.
Long on the lofty cliffs, the steep confining them within their home,
Across the void—the vaporous deep—they watched for him again to
    come.

He came not any more to them. How fared he—died—to whom
    bequeathed
His glorious realm and diadem, to us no word hath history breathed.
(Remember ye, these things befell ere Clio took in hand her style.)
What records have been found but tell the tale of this deserted isle.
Moreover, they are hard to read, and hidden from the ken of most,
Who little reck thereof; indeed, for them they are as good as lost.

Albeit, he who had bereft this tribe of help and rule benign,
On many a monument had left his cypher set in deep design;
And wrought devices that displayed far-seeing and judicious care
In divers plans right deftly laid to make their island safe and fair.
Innumerable proofs remained—some plain to all, some buried far—
That there, in ages past, had reigned one wiser than our wisest are.

The generation that had seen the splendours of his sovereignty
Passed from the earth; their sons might glean somewhat of how it used
    to be,
But as these dwindled, year by year, that period and that king became
First a bright memory, then a mere tradition, then naught but a name.
The all-sufficient code he framed, since it had been but day by day
And only orally proclaimed, soon slipt from all men's minds away.

Yet still one law—one primal rule, well called of gold—nay (for it lights
The dim soul of the veriest fool, and glimmers for the blindest wights)
Of purest diamond-crystal, say, set indestructible, a gem
Flashing sure guidance with a ray unquenchable—illumined them,
Or would, had they but followed it, and dealt in all things as it led;
So simple to the dullest wit, yet in its scope unlimited.

Though there it shone amid the dark for any to discern that would,
Long years elapsed and none did mark that relic in close neighbourhood ;
Until some honest soul by strong conflicting impulses perplext,
Fain to do right and shun the wrong, yet by misgivings sadly vext,
'Mid many pathways puzzled sore, and wandering as in a maze,
Urged this and that way—straight before him suddenly beheld it blaze.

Right glad he called unto his kin—the seekers, thinkers, and the sage
(For such lived, surely, even in that rude and unenlightened age).
These gathered, curious, round the prize, and one, a patriarch, hale
    though hoar,
Close scanning it with eager eyes, exclaimed, " Behold 'tis graven o'er !
It bears the very seal of him—the cypher-royal of that wise one
Of olden time, whereof our dim and differing traditions run.

" We know this signet ; we have conned it set on many a beauteous
    thing,
Of marvel and of awe beyond our ken and our interpreting.
But see ! this lies within our reach ; we grasp it, and on every side
Its flash illuminates, for each a revelation and a guide.
How many a dark and crookèd path had this made plain and luminous !
Who sayeth now that king, in wrath departing, had forgotten us ?"

So the wise ones their fellows taught that first of rules to understand ;
And, finding it so good, they sought for other tokens from that hand ;
And others found they by and by ; but deeper hid, and needing more
Skill to decipher and apply the signs and principles they bore ;
In course of time these, too, became diffused and known among them all,
Giving them handicraft to frame fair things from rough material.

So cities did they build, where lay the swamp and wilderness of weeds ;
Right goodly structures fashioned they, adapted deftly to their needs,
Wrought wondrously in wood and stone, changing the aspect of the
    earth,

So that their fathers had not known 'twas the same land that gave them
  birth.
So grew and flourished they ; but ne'er a higher law, a better plan,
Unto those islanders was e'er revealed for man to deal with man.

Yet those who have explored their isle, and studied all their works and
  ways,
Declare them prone to greed and guile ; and doubt if in these later days
Their sum of happiness be more (though proud and prosperous they be)
Than under that old King before he disappeared beyond the sea ;
Because that primal rule, though plain 'twas writ for all, scarce any keep,
So do they work each other's bane, and make the weaker ones to weep.

A foolish race, to suffer such a martyrdom of pain and grief !
Though duped, still credulous, they clutch at this and that to find relief ;
Their idols, e'en their gods they change, throning—disthroning them
  at will,
And some may be of a sort most strange ; these help not, nor can stay
  the ill.
Poor sufferers ; within each one lieth the remedy ; for sure
Themselves have wrought their woes, and none but they themselves can
  work the cure.

A SONG FOR MY SON.

TAKE, my son, upon thy journey this memorial of me ;
In the race and in the tourney let this token be for thee
Not the mere words of thy father—the reflection of *his* thought ;
Old world-truths long patent, rather, taken from rich mines, and wrought
Into missive form to win thee from the Specious to the True,
And to stir thy soul within thee to pursue and cleave thereto.

Dowered or no with ample measure at capricious Fortune's hands—
Blessed or no with ease and leisure, if thou'lt but discern, there stands
One attendant at thy shoulder, One to thy young eyes, maybe,
Seemingly of aspect colder than the others beckoning thee.
If that One thou wilt but follow, she shall gift thee more than all ;
When all else hath proved but hollow, her delights shall never pall.

Take her hand ; for she will light thee unto many a treasure-store,
And for all thy pains requite thee, though the toil thereto be sore.
She with runic song will charm thee on the march and at the halt ;
And she none the less will arm thee for defence and for assault
With the weaponry thou needest for the battle-day to come,
If her tutelage thou heedest, nor forsak'st as burdensome.

So thy monitress shall dip thee in her waters by the heel,
And, invulnerate, equip thee—but with other gear than steel.
For the slayer and the smiter hath not honour as of yore ;
'Tis the keen and cogent writer swayeth peoples more and more ;
By the singer and the speaker shall humanity be stirred,
And armaments prove weaker than the lightnings of their word.

*   *   *   *   *   *

Heed, my son, heed that thou givest keen attention to the Tale
Of the land wherein thou livest, piercing through the specious veil
Woven by ingenious writers, glittering-hued and gem-bedecked,
Gaudy-wrought with crowns and mitres ; peer beyond this, and detect
How—in what plight fared the many, while the prideful, ravening few
Strove for kingship ; let not any pageantry obstruct thy view.

Sycophancy o'er that Story hath a dazzling glamour flung,
Hiding in a haze of glory (so yclept to lure the young)
Murder, rapine, lust, and plunder of defenceless, harmless folk ;
Dastard ruffianism under kingly robe and ermined cloak ;
Ruthless grinding of the tillers and the toilers and the meek,
Usurpation by the killers and the spoilers of the weak.

Chroniclers these things indited (whether by design or no),
So the shallow and short-sighted give no thought to look below,
'Neath the blazonry concealing grievous wrongs and cruelties ;
Read *thou* them with heart and feeling, not with mere scholastic eyes.
Recollect, too, in an age when few could read, and fewer write,
Fewer still dared pen a page unpleasing to the monarch's sight.

From such partisan narration copyists have handed down
Unto each young generation the tradition of a crown
By its contact sanctifying ; so, for any crownèd thing—
Dolt, poltroon, or God-denying lunatic—once throned as King,
At his sovereign will and pleasure sorrowing men must toil and bleed,
Yielding up their lives and treasure to subserve his pride and greed.

This, that Tale, as mostly writ, perpetuates in youthful minds;
Compassion is benumbed by it; the common herd, the serfs and hinds,
To eyes of embryo Chathams are of small account as grains of sand,
By King and Kaiser, Queen and Czar tossed easily from hand to hand.
So surviveth the idea—thus ever nourishēd anew—
That God ordained the earth to be a portion for the prideful few.

Most tenacious that tradition, though with million evils fraught;
Breeding slaves whose manumission is but slowly, hardly bought.
Right Divine! The first king given—Saul—(say Books that cannot lie)
Was sent to mark the wrath of Heaven; with monition from on high
Warning of the traits of royal anointed ones—their gentle ways.
Loyalty! Yea, my son, be loyal to Conscience only all thy days.

Are, then, all men equal? No; for none to rule and none be ruled,
Things were ne'er designēd so; but be ye not by phrases fooled.
Sovereignty is to the strongest, that is so, and aye will be;
Once 'twas he of sharpest, longest sweep of sword and war-axe—he
Who, his way to kingship winning by his courage, proved his claim;
So it was in the beginning; 'tis the same now—yet not the same.

Who governeth, who beareth sway, unto whom do the people yield?
Not the gilt manikins that play with weaponry they cannot wield:
Not the small puppets tricked in gauds and robes belonging to the Great,
Whom hungry Opulence applauds, expectant, at the palace-gate.
The sovereign power that moveth men these weaklings cannot stay nor
    stem,
'Tis nigh maturity, and then—lo, it shall make an end of them.

Look thou discerningly, and see how Forms whereout the life has fled
Do exercise authority and awe the multitude, though dead:
Until the slowly-gathering storm in hearts of men that hate deceit
Breaks fierce, and sweeps away the Form that was but hollow and a
    cheat.
So shall the new supplant the old that hath become corrupt and foul;
Help thou the fabric to re-mould which shelters but the bat and owl.

*   *   *   *   *   *

The order of the world is change—'tis trite as two and two are four ;
Yet but in form, an aspect strange but masks phenomena, no more.
Say some : " All truth has been foretold ; naught can be better than our
     best ;
Unto one faith the soul must hold as final, else are we unblest."
Grasp thou *this* truth, as old as time, yet blinked and blinked from age
     to age—
From the first quickening mass of slime all things have grown from stage
     to stage.

Of genesis, keen search hath solved thus much for us: We know that One
From protoplasmic pulp evolved such types as graced the Parthenon.
As in primordial forms, brute Strength—blind, blundering, cruel—won
     foremost place,
Till, after countless æons, at length, wide-eyed, endued with skill and
     grace—
Nay, majesty, the tawny king roamed peerless, mighty-voiced and grand,
At sound whereof each living thing quailed, knowing none might him
     withstand ;

So 'mong the psychal forces, blind conglomerated embryons,
That swam in dimly pregnant mind (when our far sires were but the
     sons
Of anthropoids) the first of all that came to perfect form and birth
Was that grand quality we call by name of Courage ; and its worth,
Right quickly recognised, made chief him that did most thereof display ;
Yet 'twas but as an outer leaf within whose folds *all* virtue lay.

These first-born twins by right shall rule ; for where men dwell the truth
     will hold
That there will also dwell the fool, the dastard, and the sordid-souled :
These twain, but under other forms more subtle and less gross, shall
     reign,

What revolutionary storms soe'er may rage, what gods be slain.
These two the peoples so applaud—so heartily revere as true,
They even bow before the gaud and garb that appertain thereto.

He of the loyalest heart, and who with readiest love and sacrifice
Doeth sincerest homage to the truly Great and Strong and Wise,
At mumming counterfeits thereof the sharper-barbĕd shaft will wing ;
The quicker gibe, the louder scoff, and the more bitter taunt will fling
When Littleness, Ineptitude, and stolid Selfishness are seen
With royal insignia endued, and aping the majestic mien.

He that doth most revere the High, the Holy, the Sublime, the True,
More keenly and more jealously—with closer scrutiny doth view
The idols set before his eyes and shrined for his adoring gaze ;
And if discerned for falsities, in sharper scorn, in fiercer blaze
Of anger doth his soul outbreak : him the more mighty impulse stirs
To overturn them, and awake their duped and drowsy worshippers.

But bethink thee, when a nation deems it fortunate indeed,
Braying fulsome adulation of its monarch if he lead
But a life of due abstention from the scandalous and vile ;
As 'twere gracious condescension if he do not *more* defile
The regalia than his fathers, and but stay the hand malign :
Such the royalist beslathers with laudation nigh divine.

See, if the sovereign do but feign propriety, th' idolaters shout
Pæans in nauseating strain ; if she do but display throughout
A decent, inoffensive life the graces of the homeliest dame,
The virtues of the humblest wife, and do no flagrant deed of shame,
In grateful admiration prone, the pack of cringing flunkeys cry,
" Sure ne'er was such illustrious one as this—our demi-deity !"

See the servile—always loyal—acclaim with blatant, flattering breath
One bedecked in trappings royal, with naught of regal underneath ;
One who reigneth but by reason of collateral descent

From a plotter of high treason to the people : he had rent,
Save for thwarting, into tatters the thin fabric of their rights,
Leaving care of kingly matters to licentious parasites.

One whose right to rule derives through yet another's tainted blood,
E'en that king whose name survives, a synonym for dastard-hood ;
Genius hath the record graven of that doubly treacherous one,
Verily the falsest craven that did e'er pollute a throne ;
More contemptible defacer of the scutcheon of his race—
Blacker-hearted one and baser ne'er did squat in Alfred's place.

A right deriving through a strain but little purer than of these ;
That of a scion called to reign, yet half afraid to cross the seas
To guard his faithful people's weal—of such a kingly sort was he ;
Nor wit nor heart, nor soul to feel the sacrament of sovereignty ;
A libertine, and of the worst—the cold, ungallant, churlish breed ;
First of the alien kings that cursed this land with most prolific seed.

And in his train there flocked at beck the jay, the vulture, and the kite ;
With hungry eye and craning neck they followed, scenting spoil ; a
    flight
Of famished harpies, from their nigh-exhausted feeding-grounds un-
    cooped,
Chuckling—in gutturals—to descry a prey so fat and foolish, swooped,
With keen tenacious talons, swift upon these fair and fruitful lands ;
And highest place was bribe or gift from George's blowsy harlot's
    hands.

On, through his progeny, devolves th' insignia that in the eyes
Of miscalled loyalty absolves from all that sovereignty implies.
To re-narrate the lives and rule of these anointed ones would be
To stir a fœtid sewage-pool—a foul, unlovely work : but we
Are bidden to behold with pride the constitutional device
Whereby their seed are sanctified.   Say, Demos, are they worth their
    price ?

No spark of heroism, no gleam of genius—nay, of intellect—
Did one display to half redeem their negligence ; 'mong these elect
There stood no right true man, much less a leader and a chief of men :
Nameless, unbridled lecherousness, the cock-pit and the gambling den,
The brutal pugilistic duel—such were the pastimes of them all ;
Finding their sport but in the cruel, their pleasure in the sensual.

There reigned not one whose soul aspired above the sordid and the
  coarse :
Ignoble, bestial, they bemired the fount of honour at its source,
So that the taint thereof became contagious even to the best ;
Since they that bore the kingly name were creatures the unkingliest—
The dolt, the sot, the debauchee, the coxcomb, and the gamester-cheat ;
Strength, Courage, Genius—these royal three were thrust for such from
  Harold's seat.

Through such devolves this sacred right—this subtle, sanctifying grace,
Unto this last ; and, lo, a sight—a sham enthroned in Wisdom's place,
With dandy-sycophants set round to intercept the vulgar groan.
Since Sloth and Avarice are crowned, needs must be Valour mocked—
  for one
Brutal-tongued as craven-hearted, star-bedizened, struts and swells
In the garb of a departed hero, brave, if nothing else.

Mark ye that alien race ; with one tradition are they all imbued,
For subjects fraught with evils uncomputable in magnitude.
All of that line were from their birth upon one baneful fiction fed ;
That though for most be dole and dearth, long labour-ache and lack of
  bread,
There must no due nor tribute fail to fill *their* goblet to the brim,
Though the rich wine be pressed by pale emaciate Misery hunger-grim :

That there must be for *them* no lack of splendour or emolument,
Though men be mad with want, and black each heart and brow with
  discontent :
That though the outcry of distress make sad the sunlight, there must be

No gaud, no gem, no plume the less to grace their glittering pageantry :
That peoples live to pleasure them—not they to guard the people's weal,
The flood of human ills to stem, the mass of misery to heal.

The care that chiefly stirreth these royal dullards to activity
Is to make safe and hide the keys of their vast wealth from scrutiny ;
Possessions filched from a befooled and blinded people in the past,
When common rights were over-ruled ; when Brunswick's swarm of
        harpies cast
Rapacious glance o'er many a wide and fair demesne, and clutched at
        them,
Seizing, with claim quick ratified ; and none did dare the theft condemn.

The least of their concerns, the last to trouble their repose serene,
Is care for those whose lives are passed in constant jeopardy between
The wolf that must be stayed within, and vampires threatening from
        without ;
Who, pinching, toil and, sorrowing, spin unceasingly, in carking doubt
Of how to win the morrow's meal.   Such be not kingly cares ; yet loyal
Should workers be, and proud, as leal purveyors to the Stomach Royal !

One instinct only, but one thought, did and doth dominate them all—
To grasp and to retain, but naught bestow ; nay, making constant call,
With most imperial impudence, upon the toilers' little store
To add to their magnificence and their aggrandisement the more.
A vulgar and a vulturous line ! nor true nor firm in anything—
Save to insist on their divine prerogative of plundering.

Shall a system of succession giving unto such as these
Richest realms for a possession hold a nation to its knees ?
Shall the profligate inherit them, the miser, and the fool,
It being held as merit that they do but feign to rule ?
Shall the shades of tyrants buried fleece us through their feeble sons ?
Give thy answer from the serried ranks of the rebellious ones.

A SONG FOR MY SON.

Be it thine to swell the number crying out on every hand—
Shall this heavy thing encumber any more the weary land?
Be it thine to join the others who have pondered on the wrong,
And to animate thy brothers, for the battle will be long.
Seek thy place among their forces, gathering silently but fast,
With thy talents, thy resources, all the faculties thou hast;

Striving so to scatter seedful truths abroad that they shall bring
The unthinking to grow heedful, till they recognise this thing —
This begilded idol standing open-mouthed and hungry-mawed,
Tribute, tithe, and toll demanding, fed by statutory fraud—
To be futile, false, and hollow; so to undermine its base
That they who are to follow thee shall drag it from its place.

    *   *   *   *   *   *

Living, as thou dost, possessing liberty of thought and deed,
See thou valuest that blessing, for 'twas won right hardly; heed
Whose high heroism wrought it—aye, and mark *in spite of whom ;*
Whose self-sacrifices bought it, though at price of fiery doom;
Who maintained it 'gainst incessant royal encroachment, subtly planned,
And bequeathed it to the present—us their children, this their land.

Mark the foes thereof, gigantic truly—ravening Greed and Pride,
And Another, belching frantic malediction far and wide.
Mark her well, for thou wilt meet her at each step of thy advance,
E'en through life; but, to unseat her champion, needs but tip thy lance
With the crystal Truth she hateth, 'tis the thing she most doth fear;
Yet must watch, for aye she waiteth to attack thee from the rear.

Ere our fathers (as thou learnest) brake their fetters link by link,
Time was when the studious, earnest seekers, all who dared to think,
And to speak the thought that stirred them, though 'twere only under
    breath,
Were it *new*, had need to gird them for a conflict to the death
With a monster keen as ruthless, quick in craft as cruel of hand:
Thou but seest her tottering, toothless, and this canst not understand.

Thou art free to think and utter whatsoe'er thou deemest right ;
But did thy forefathers mutter truths now popular and trite,
Quick as panther and as direful in ferocity—nay, more,
Straight upon them sprang an ireful Church that never then forbore—
Were it suckling mother, tender maid, or prattling little one—
In her savage hate to rend her victims limb from limb ere done.

Thou art free to love thy brother, and to fare with him as thine,
Though he worship at another and, to thee, an unknown shrine.
This is worth thy recognition, for it was not always so—
It *had* wrought thy soul's perdition, nor so very long ago ;
If to such thou hadst but given food and drink for kinhood's sake,
Thou hadst lost thy hopes of Heaven—it had brought thee to the stake !

Look around thee, and thou seest fearless, open-mannered folk ;
If thou to their thought agreest not, thine own thou needst not cloak.
Long as thou dost naught offensive to thy fellows' sense or weal,
Thou needst not be apprehensive, and thy deed or word conceal :
Neither monarch nor his minion, priest nor titled popinjay,
Dare disturb thee for opinion uttered in the public-way.

Slow, to this, hath been our progress ; only since the realm was rent
From the clutches of that Ogress, hateful, yet omnipotent,
And her sorcerous fortress shaken, were the people's eyes unsealed,
Did the minds of men awaken ; for the tyrant's doom had pealed—
Pealed, but ere the retribution be exacted to the full,
Ere the day of restitution, long the strife and terrible.

Slow, through outrage, dole, and slaughter, our deliverance, even since ;
For the Hag's misgotten daughter, harlot to a lecher-prince,
Sitting throned but little lower than the mother sat before,
Proved as pitiless in power, wreaking penalties as sore ;
And, as in succubœan dream, the wise discerned a monstrous thing—
God's Truth revised, maintained supreme by grace of an ungodly king !

But the shrewd were set a-thinking, witnessing a thing so odd ;
Wakeful, once fooled by a winking Virgin and a wafer-God,
Sundry of them 'gan to search, and e'en to eye the Book askant :
There might be a king and Church exchanging winks significant !
Thus strange doubts were set abrew, since now it was declared enough
To hold the doctrine stamped as true by such an one as Butcher Bluff !

Search, nor cease till thou hast mastered all the story of this time,
Spite of glozers of that dastard crowned embodiment of crime.
Mark the hybrid Church that flung its shadow o'er the people's homes—
The blood-sodden soil whence sprung its roots : its victims' catacombs
Are underneath it ; and, above, the fumes of burning flesh lie dense.
Yet will thy teachers maunder of its " civilising influence."

*   *   *   *   *   *

Thou must needs be keen to sunder fact from fable ; when thou hast,
Thou wilt clearly see that under mighty empires in the past
(For thee, as the Tale thou connest, re-arising from their dust),
Long as men were truthful, honest, sober, merciful, and just,
Free were they to make oblation to that form of the Divine
Worthiest of their adoration—that they deemed the holiest shrine,

Where or whatsoe'er conceived they the Omnipotent to be ;
Whatso'er ideal believed they truest, worshipped they.   Thus free
Were the peoples till that day when there appeared in Eastern lands,
Girt with spears and armed array, a Symbol borne by bloody hands ;
And its heralds, stern and dolorous, showed thereon a legend writ,
Of a sort to catch the timorous, and to win the weak of wit ;

Of a sort to breed deniers of a righteous Judge on high ;
To beget a race of liars feigning to believe a lie ;
To engender strife ; to deaden pity in the human soul ;
Smiling lands to blast and redden, turning gladness into dole ;
Hearts of men to break or harden wheresoe'er its shadow fell,
Till it filled our Father's Garden with the flames and shrieks of Hell ;

Till the earth, for most, became a place of horror and despair,
And the highest, holiest Name a name to curse with only ; ne'er
Theretofore had persecution, deaf to ruth and frenzy-blind,
Wrought such havoc and pollution in the conscience of mankind.
Ne'er wept the world so, seeing done such bloody work at human hands ;
Nay, through Time's glass had never run such ruddy and tear-sodden
    sands !

Thou wilt see that mankind oweth these things to a cursèd creed ;
Wherefrom, surely as there groweth deadly bane from hemlock-seed,
Issued forth a raging devil armed with torch and rack and rod ;
Hear it :— *Work he good or evil, man shall not be judged of God*
By the things that he achieveth ; nay, his soul shall live or die
By the things that he believeth, and be blessed or banned thereby.   .

Herein, as close-coiled within the cobra's egg lies poison-death,
Lurks the baneful origin of madnesses whereat the breath
Chokes in utterance.   Mark and ponder well the outcome of that Lie :
All the beauty, all the wonder writ for us 'twixt earth and sky,
Set as secret lessons, hidden only that they may be sought,
All became a book forbidden, harbouring a demon—Thought.

Foul and fanged and fast-engendered crawled its offspring o'er the earth,
Vilifying all that rendered human life of any worth ;
Smiting, numbing, and besliming, with envenomed tooth and tongue,
All man's faculties for climbing up beyond the mists that hung
O'er his spiritual being at the dawning of his mind—
God-gifts for his own self-freeing from the woes of humankind.

All his blessèd, wondrous dower of loving heart and subtle brain,
All his glorious, mystic power of intellect they would have slain,
Had these things not been of Heaven ; mingled with but mortal clay,
Crushed and trampled (but as leaven, ever working weal), they lay
Stricken, fearful of betraying stir of thought or sign of life,
Neither song nor speech essaying, for the horror that was rife.

See the deadly poison lurking in that fatalest of creeds ;
Trace the virus spreading, working ; the malignant things it breeds,
Multiform and pestilential ; see, at last, these coalesced ;
Witness, then, an all-potential monster rear its hydra crest,
All the tyrannies uniting to itself, and with its breath
Making foul the earth, and blighting souls with spiritual death.

Mark : its dupe, his mind infected, paralysed, and made afraid,
In his mad mistrust rejected, as insidious, the aid
Wherewithal his God supplied him, his equipment for the fight
Given to sustain and guide him in his struggle t'wards the light :
So that he became a creature cowering as if under ban,
Terror-struck, with scarce a feature of the brave and honest Man.

For dominant, and clad with might, behold this Incubus, the Church,
Loud-denying him his right to freely reason, think, and search ;
Aye, his right inalienable, to discern by fearless quest
Whether tales be fact or fable, whether things abide the test
Furnished for his self-protection, set within his heart and soul
For a safeguard and direction through the mists that hide his goal.

Rights, these, that by man may never be surrendered but with shame ;
Duties, these, that whosoever shirks and delegates—the same
Doth do so at his peril ; yea, the tyrant king and priest shall grind
And devour him as their prey ; him soul and body shall they bind,
Strip and yoke to serve their lust : nor shall the gods be pitiful,
But leave such craven in the dust, degraded and contemptible.

What but trial and search incessant, and audacious questioning,
From the dim Past to the Present, hath availed man anything ?
Pensively his gaze projecting over earth and into space,
Fearlessly the false detecting—truly 'twas by *these* our race
Won its victories and mounted arduously, stage by stage,
Through the centuries uncounted from the first strong Thinker's age.

The primeval man that cowered ape-like in his dwelling-place,
Rock-hewn cave or nest embowered, but beheld Panthea's face
Dark with menace ; he but saw around, below and overhead,
Threatening forms of fear and awe, but phantoms dire and forces dread :
Lightning-bolt and thunder-crash, keen winter's biting blast and stress,
Were as foes that seemed to dash their strength against his nakedness.

Plagues and evils that attacked him—famine, drought, and pestilence ;
Maladies and pains that racked him, aidless in his impotence ;
Havoc of the fearsome quaking, cracking earth beneath his feet ;
Ruin of the storm-cloud breaking, wrapping him with flaming sheet ;
Fire and flood that left him bare of shelter and bereft of kin—
These for æons cowed him ere the first true seer discerned therein

The inscrutable Creator's emissaries grim and stern,
High-commissioned inculcators of the precept—" Seek and Learn !
Seek throughout thy habitation, search thine whole environment ;
All its deep interpretation learn thou, and let none prevent !
All to sense or soul existent put thou sharply to the proof ;
Search and scrutiny persistent—ply *these* for thine own behoof."

These the ministers that scourged him into effort self-reliant ;
This the mandate high that urged him to investigate, defiant
Of the cunning fetish-monger and the cursing mystery-man ;
Servile to their craft no longer, nor obeisant to their ban,
Strove he, baffling their endeavour to intimidate his mind ;
Else had he remained forever destitute, abased, and blind.

Ours had been a story bare of soaring thought and lofty deed
Had our fathers failed to dare the priestly ban, and given heed
To the cursing crew that bade them search no farther.   But behold,
He whose ancestor, skin-clad, nomadic roamed the woods and wold,
Hunger-driven, making war with plaited noose and flint-stone axe,
Hath linked the levin to his car, and scaled the heights of parallax.

Look back, in imagination, to the twilight of his prime—
From thy safe and hard-won station to the uncomputed time
When he, on his first awaking to the powers that lay in him,
From the bonds of terror breaking, into the assailants grim
That so harassed and pursued him, shot the arrows of his thought,
Fronting them that erst subdued him with his weapons newly wrought.

When he had discerned the sources of his maladies and woes—
Found the elemental forces not to be malignant foes,
But benign, though minatory, agents pliant to his skill—
Grown resourceful, deft, no more he cowered when they wrought him ill ;
Seeing in their tumult other than consuming wrath and death ;
Learning that the bounteous Mother for our weal thus laboureth.

Then arose that spectral Terror 'mong the peoples to condemn
Energy and Thought as error, cursing and arresting them.
'Neath its hateful domination man, distraught by new alarms,
At its tyrannous dictation flung aside his proper arms ;
Conscience, test of reason, these he straight abandoned for its creed,
So that he became an easy prey to priestly craft and greed.

Though the bigotry that brought him to such pass is yet alive
In the Church that aye hath taught him but to suffer—not to strive ;
Ever, since she drilled and schooled him not to question, but obey ;
Ever, since the Fathers fooled him, since the pontiffs held their sway—
Playing, in the name of Heaven, the lecher, murderer, and thief—
Hath his progress been the even measure of his disbelief. ·

Disbelief that revelation lit but one—the Hebrew race ;
Disbelief in a salvation by capricious act of grace ;
In man's pre-ordained perdition ere he issued from the womb ;
In a priest's divine commission to assign reward or doom ;
In a Deity demanding of His creatures—tyrant-wise,
Reason, Thought, and Understanding slain as grateful sacrifice.

So far as he hath rejected these things, and his mind thereof
Cleared and purged and disinfected (spite of pharisaic scoff),
Just *so* far is he enabled to pursue his quest for Truth,
And to read aright the fabled stories of his planet's youth ;
Verily to love his neighbour, though in thrall to idols base ;
And undauntedly to labour for the welfare of his race.

As his old false beacon crumbled, and its red glare flickered dim,
So with a more truly humbled spirit hath he worshipped Him ;
More devoutly sought His presence, and more duly kept His law ;
Leaving theories of His essence for the dogmatist to draw—
Heir of the patristic spiders that with futile labour spun,
Analysers and dividers of the High and Holy One.

In so far as he hath broken from the bondage of that Creed,
Freely searched and thought and spoken, fearing not nor giving heed
To the Church's curse—the flaming torture here and afterward ;
Lies, though crowned, *as* lies proclaiming, by their menace undebarred ;
So far hath he rendered fertile regions barren heretofore,
Ploughing up the tangled, sterile waste of " theologic " lore ;

Through its murky labyrinth clearing pathways unto regions new,
Into daylight pioneering seekers of the high and true ;
Judging with a wider vision of his future by his past ;
Wak'ning to his true position in the universal vast ;
Loftiest peak and deepest ocean forcing to declare their tale,
And the stellar atoms, motion measuring by rule and scale.

As his mind refused submission to the yoke, and dared rebel,
It regained its strength—volition, paralysed beneath that spell ;
It uprose, re-animated, from its servitude to fear,
And his soul was liberated from the dungeon dark and drear
Builded by his crafty masters to obscure it and confine,
And devised that so his pastors might distort the Light divine.

As he hath escaped that prison, and his captors hath defied,
So he hath advanced and risen ; nay, the more he hath denied
Credence to his priestly teachers, more he hath been just and kind
Unto all his fellow-creatures, with a justice unconfined
To one sect or race or nation ; with a mercy unwithheld
E'en from him who seeks salvation elsewise than from books of eld ;

Elsewise than in basest barter—as the price of guiltless blood ;
Yielding to the Peasant-Martyr but the claims of brotherhood ;
Thinking not to buy redemption whensoever he hath erred ;
Seeking not to win exemption from the penalties incurred—
To escape the retribution following with unfaltering tread
By a dastard substitution of another in his stead.

As he hath revolted, turning in deep loathing from that Lie,
So have cultivation, learning—all the useful arts whereby
Human suffering and affliction find relief—made speedier way ;
For the Church's malediction and her forces' whole array
Ever have been set to bar the march of all that maketh free—
Ever hath she striv'n to mar the dawning smile of Liberty.

Study well the annals—pages blood-writ and aglare with flame—
Of her empire through the ages of her undisputed claim ;
When all Christendom obeyed the voice of her as voice of God,
When, omnipotent, she swayed the destinies thereof, and trod
On the necks of prince and Cæsar—aye, with courtesy sharp and scant,
Swiftly bringing to their knees her vassal-kings recalcitrant.

With dominion unresisted, with authority supreme,
Binding, loosing as she listed, oh, what grand and glorious dream
Had been realised for waiting, suffering mortals, even here,
Had she striv'n towards abating sorrow in this lower sphere !
Feeble Right had never yielded unto Wrong's tyrannic might
Had her armèd strength been wielded as *its* champion in the fight.

The chivalry of Europe leapt her beck and bidding to obey ;
Had but her uplifted sceptre been the signal, in that day,
Not for her too zealous legions, led by Craft and urged by Greed,
To invade and plunder regions unenlightened by her creed,
But to set the weak and lowly victims of the despot free,
All had testified the Holy Spirit moved her verily !

Thus enthroned, and in her hands the keys of Heaven and of Hell,
Clothed with power unchallenged—stands the record that she used it
    well ?
Witness, ye who perished under cruelest torments at her hands—
In the furnace, torn asunder—rise and speak, ye, from the lands
In the old days given over to her for a pastorate,
From the hallowed graves that cover you, the brave, the wise, the great !

Bear your witness, O ye sainted victims of her ruthless might,
Whom her virulence attainted of the crime of seeking light—
Crime of groping upwards through the blackest night the world hath
    known ;
When right loud and piteous grew the universal sob and groan :
When o'er every homestead hovered shadows fraught with fire and doom,
And when Learning's lamp was covered, quenched in sacerdotal gloom :

When at every hearth sat terror, lest the father, wife, or son
Were accused, suspect of error, and their gladsome days were done ;
Lest, unwittingly, by word light-spoken, they perchance had strayed,
And quick Spite had overheard, rejoicing, so they were betrayed
To the Church's cruel purgation—to the torture (ne'er the less
Wrought she thus by inspiration of the God of Righteousness !) :

When fanatical Suspicion lurked alike in cot and hall,
And the Holy Inquisition shed a horror over all ;
For it spread a net so none might hope to hide beyond its reach,
Nor escape the toils it spun for snaring wingèd Thought and Speech—
Subtly set to trap and strangle such in whatsoever guise,
And of purpose to entangle Knowledge in a web of lies.

Bear your witness, O ye martyrs done to death—but not o'erawed,
Were not her Decretal charters forgeries, and based on fraud?
This the monkish scribes oft muttered in their cups, but ne'er avowed
Till the patent fact was uttered in the market-place, aloud:
Say, ye, if by *her* endeavour Truth and Justice might prevail—
Witness, ye! or did she ever fight against them tooth and nail?

Do they tell thee I am railing at a phantom of the past,
And but foolishly assailing one who long ago was cast
Out from her assumed dominion: one whom those she sought to harm
Have been fortunate to pinion, disentitle, and disarm;
One now moribund, and bearing rule no more for peace or strife,
Ghastly-hideous only, wearing but similitude of life?

Who is this, be-mitred, standing but a step below the throne,
Swol'n, gold-gorged—yet more demanding—what is this proud-visaged
    one
But that ancient tyrant's daughter—yea, her own true child is she,
Albeit the angry beldame brought her forth in hate, abortively;
For this offspring doth inherit all the jealous arrogance—
All the persecuting spirit that hath barred mankind's advance.

On her front she bears the nævus—aye, her prideful parent's mark,
And her rule had been as grievous, merciless, malign, and dark,
But that our brave fathers slipt the meshes round about them spun;
Challenged, vanquishèd, and stript her of her weapons one by one.
Though she feigneth well—beware! her cursings, petulant and shrill,
Tell us how the world would fare had she the power to work her will.

All the subtleties devised to awe, bewilder, and delude,
Whereby the Mother terrorised the superstitious multitude;
All th' accumulated lore—the pious falsehoods, forgeries,
Frauds and fables—all her store of craftily-designèd lies,
Wrought and writ to fright unlearnèd, credulous, and simple folk,
Hath the cunning daughter turnèd to account, to fit her yoke

On the indolent successors of the earnest men who taught
Their papistical oppressors not to harass honest thought.
She hath flourished, for a season, for the populace are loth
To re-vindicate their Reason, lain for centuries in sloth ;
And the many, at the present, murmur drowsily her cant—
Are but dully acquiescent where our sires were protestant.

Like her parent, she hath striven aye to practise on their fears ;
Like her parent, she hath thriven on their blood and sweat and tears ;
Like her, she hath sought to darken every beacon save her own.
As ye love your freedom, hearken and take heed—mistrust the crone !
Blindly-stubborn is her temper, sanguined is her banner's hue,
Haughty is her crest, and "*Semper eadem*" her legend true.

Search her record : In each movement tending to the commonweal,
To enlightenment, improvement in the arts to soothe and heal,
Check disease, and overcome it ; or to free our fellow man ;
Or, when from some hard-won summit, keen explorers in the van,
Beyond her narrow ken, discovered tracks to guide or lights to cheer,
She hath lagged behind and hovered, shrieking curses, in the rear.

Mark her method now : Thou notest when the vanguard hath prevailed
'Spite her savage ban and protest, and the innovation, hailed
Far and wide with acclamation, thriveth, an established thing—
To a purblind generation, heedless of her hindering,
She (whom, truly, nothing shameth), having wrought her best and worst
To retard and damn it, claimeth to have blessed it from the first !

Do they tell thee I but fight a hoary and disabled foe—
E'en as he that doth but smite a wounded giant, stricken low :
For she, though diseased and dying, certain service wrought of yore,
Hospice and relief supplying when the earth was given o'er
For apportionment among the fiercest hearts and sharpest swords ;
When the strongest—they that swung the mightiest blades—became its
     lords ?

That her word was to contentious, savage rulers as a law
When none other the licentious, predatory hordes might awe :
Preaching Peace—Goodwill, as ne'er such message had been preached
before,
Daring all things to declare the symbol and the word she bore :
Fair-built sanctuaries founding 'mid a rough world's strife and clash,
'Mid the ravaged lands resounding ever with the battle-crash ?

That her walled domains afforded for the studious and the sage
Sheltered safe-guard 'mong the hoarded wealth of the Augustan age ;
Lodgment for the priceless olden scrolls wherein the few might seek
Lore and solace in the golden wisdom of the lucid Greek ;
Refuge and retreat for weary sinners in her cloistered shades,
So their last days were less dreary, passed among her glebes and glades ?

Do they tell thee this same Power, gigantic-looming, seeming-cruel,
Made a citadel and tower for Peace and Love, while dubious duel—
Truth 'gainst Falsehood, Right 'gainst Might—was waged before a
passive God ;
That its champions turned the fight, and, lo, where'er its legions trod
The holy, final Truth dispelled the darkness for mistaken men ;
Thought, grown presumptuous, was quelled : so He made bright His
face again ?

Do they bid thee, in the manner of this Faith's apologists,
Mark the progress of its banner ; its emergence from the mists,
Dubious, fabulous, concealing its first consecration, till,
Triumphing, it waved o'er kneeling millions, bowed in heart and will ?
Naught but God's own grace could speed it thus, all conquering, from
its prime !
(So, e'en, will the Christian plead), and, with a confidence sublime, '

Ask what Faith inspires the powers, the foremost, mightiest of the race,
And, like a rock-built beacon, towers refulgent o'er the rest ? What
place
Upon the habitable earth hath it not reached and lit ? What land

Lying within the globe's wide girth, whose people grasped the vigorous
    hand
Its roving followers out-held, but, prospering greatly, hath become
A place, where, erst, the savage dwelled, for peaceful men to make a
    home?

Lo, the regions wild that flourished where this Church hath shed her
    seed;
Lo, the thriving peoples nourished on her sweet and gentle creed;
Lo, the honour of thy daughters and the freedom of thy sons
Are secure where'er her waters have baptised the faithful ones.
Though schismatical polluters made the stream thereof as brine,
Yet these blessings (say thy tutors) prove its fount to be divine.

'Tis a fair defence, and subtle, but it toucheth not the mark;
'Tis the method of the cuttle seeking to escape the shark,
But with a difference, e'en this :—The finny one obscures his track,
Making the enemy to miss its prey, in clouds of fluid black.
Christian, from point to point hard-pressed, getteth the sun in rear,
    and lo,
Flashing in light from heel to crest, would daze his adversary so.

Thou doughty champion, mouthing Peace and Love and Holy brother-
    hood,
Thy shield is pierced; 'twere time to cease thy sophistry.   Behold, the
    blood
Of myriad victims to thy creed hath splashed thee to the very brow;
Dost think them dead and dumb indeed?   They cry unto us even now!
That light thou deem'st about thy head—rayed down from the Eternal
    Throne,
A halo on thy banner shed—is seen for other than thine own.

That light thou takest for a sign of Grace upon the conquests won
Beneath thy Symbol, doth but shine in spite of it; yea, for that sun
Long struggled dimly ere it brake, resplendent, through the dire eclipse

That followed in thy standard's wake. That sunshine whose glad
    radiance tips
Height after height puts thee to shame ; yet, being shameless, thou,
    forsooth,
Wouldst arrogate it in the name of one thou persecutedst—Truth.

Thy Truth, *thy* Symbol (callēd thine), *thy* Revelation, and *thy* Creed !
Were these things verities divine, our plight were piteous indeed.
We know thy Church was ever wont'to slay, or, were't a deathless thing,
To steal, and claim, with brazen front, 'twas nurtured 'neath her sheltering.
Thy holy books—these he who runs may read for fabulous and forged.
Thy golden plunder—this our sons may hope to live to see disgorged.

Thy Light—*thy* precious Truth indeed ! What higher, deeper, nobler
    truths—
To guide the pilgrim, or to lead the ductile minds of babes and youths ;
To draw men from pursuit of pelf, so they shall labour for the sake
Of others rather than of self—have ever been revealed than spake
The gentle Buddha, and the wise Confucius, Plato, Socrates,
Whose wisdom shall endure when dies thy barbarous deity ? and these

But gathered up wide scattered grains, and uttered forth in speech of
    gold
The echoes of forgotten fanes come down to *them* from times untold :
Yet in beneficence and worth these are as purest gems to dross
By side of aught wherefor the earth must thank the prophets of the
    Cross.
We know thy crafty Church but thieved these gems and set them as her
    own,
Though generations have believed them to be hers and hers alone.

Of new ? She *hath* bestowed one jewel unique—yea, verily she hath !
A triune deity more cruel, more fierce in his insensate wrath,
More savage in his jealous hate than any of the idols whom

He cursed and could not tolerate; more slow to save, more swift to
    doom,
More hideously unjust to man—or virtuous or vile—and more
Ferociously vindictive than were any that had reigned before.

Thy Symbol, that thou *callest* thine, and showest unto infant eyes
As shaped in Heaven—thy God's own sign, for thee descended from
    the skies,
Ne'er sacred held before : this is but borrowed by thy Church and ta'en,
Like all her other properties, from many an ancient pagan fane
Where rose the sacrifice and psalm to Baal, Moloch, Ashtaroth ;
Zeus, Adonai, Serapis, Brahm ; Osiris, Isis, Pasht, and Thoth.

In old Phœnicia, Babylon, Etruria, Ind, and hoar Thibet,
On obelisk and pylus on the banks of farthest Nile, was set
That symbol; aye, and *there* it bore significance of fructuous life,
Unnumbered centuries before 'twas borne by her in bloodiest strife ;
Long—long before she taught mankind the proper hue thereof was red,
Its shape a hilted blade designed the blood of infidels to shed.

Her scriptures, she would teach our youth, were writ by trembling scribes
    the while
God's awful voice pealed forth His truth, and His own hand did guide
    the style,
His lightnings playing o'er the scroll made holy by His very word ;
He sealing with His seal the whole ! Yea, every child that tale hath
    heard
From lips of Christian priest, and tongue of minister most sanctified,
Charged by thy Church to train the young in truthful ways—and thus
    they lied.

Her new Evangel, she would teach, was writ by apostolic hands—
By sainted witnesses, who each fared forth o'er the Judæan sands
Ever attendant on their Lord, so every wondrous work he wrought

And every precept, word for word—remembering all, omitting naught—
They wrote upon the sacred page, e'en as 'tis set before our eyes :
So tells she them of tender age ; thus, knowingly, again she lies.

Her Gospel—by whose hands 'twas writ thou know'st no more than any
    child.
Her canon—who determined it ? Were the manifold scriptures piled
(As Pappus saith) upon the floor, the Council praying for a sign ;
When, lo, the Books Inspired leapt o'er the false, and proved themselves
    divine
By self-arrangement on the top, so were the lowermost cast out ?
This tale sufficēd, *then*, to stop the mouths of any who might doubt.

A murk, wherein the keenest miss all clue for certain guidance, lies
O'er that Jew's apotheosis, o'er the inception and the rise
Of the tradition of his life. Unknown his place and year of birth ;
'Mong the conflicting stories rife, which can we count of any worth ?
'Twas not till after centuries three that any book thereof was held
As of supreme authority, and pious faith therein compelled.

And many a zealous scribe did add thereto whate'er he deemed they
    lacked,
Portents and miracles—none forbade ; such fraud was thought a pious act.
Thou knowest thou wouldst not hang a dog upon such shadowy evidence
As thou dost fish from out that fog of fable with such diligence
To prove thy Gospel from the first was held as God's own Testament ;
Yet on such proof thy Church hath cursed all who denied 'twas Heaven-
    sent.

To terrify or to beguile those who her precious Word denied,
No artifice—no fraud so vile, so infamous but she hath plied,
No forger but whose guilt she shared. Well knoweth she the tome she
    quotes
As Holy Writ was but declared the Word of God by human votes
Eliminating from a mass of manuscript pseudonymous
The Books ye impudently pass as wrought by miracle for us.

Her Creed she putteth forth as one the Galilean did impose
On his disciples, as the Son co-eval with the Father ; those
(She would imply) did verily hear how that salvation might be bought—
Did hearken to announcement clear thereof, and reverently caught
The blessèd phrases as they fell from him in ecstasy sublime,
And so transmitted them, thus well attested, even to our time.

If shrinking from that lie direct, yet do thy priests convey the same
To children ere they can reflect from whence their Sabbath bogies came.
Canst tell us unto whom, and when, that Man e'er spake one word of it ?
Had Mary, or the Magdalen, or the first Twelve e'er heard of it ?
This creed by Heaven revealed to thee—who holds it ? who hath ever held
It in its pristine purity ? did mystic Paul when he rebelled ?

We know that 'tween the year of grace that saw the martyred Nazarene
And that when first thy creed we trace, long centuries did intervene.
We know thy formula (that binds but those whom it hath made as fools)
Was long evolving from the minds of fanatics of various schools ;
Know whose authoritative voice cried, " Quibblers, cease ! the Faith
    define !
" Ye cannot ?   Then will *I* make choice, and say what shall be held
    divine !"

We know what wranglings 'twixt enraged be-mitred disputants were rife ;
What conflict long and fierce they waged, how tigerish was their hateful
    strife
Around the quiddities thereof ; what frauds—what deeds of blood and
    shame
(Well meriting the pagan's scoff) they wrought therefor ere it became
Defined and formulated, firm established, fixed by royal decree.
We trace how, from the triple germ—Fear, Hate, and crass Credulity—

Up-grew the baneful, hideous thing—thy creed, that after centuries seven
A half-barbaric Frankish King approved as final and of Heaven !
The voices that have turned the scale in Council, voting—"False or
    True ?"

The hands that made that vote prevail, and gave thy Faith its form and .
  hue,
That shaped and set thy precious jewel, were those of savage monsters
  . . twain, ,
Most pious, infamous, and cruel—e'en Constantine and Charlemagne.

Thus through thy Church's whole career bloodguiltiness and guile are
  seen.
Slaying in fury, and in fear denying such hath ever been ;
Aye crafty to conceal the Truth—of Falsehood quick to take avail ;
These were her methods, and, in sooth, 'tis but of late they 'gan to fail.
Deceit and false pretensions—these have marked her every word and
  act ;
And this the dullest student sees when he her progress hath re-tracked.

*　　*　　*　　*　　*　　*

Saladin's sword had slept in sheath, nor had the sceptic cared to cast
These wickednesses in the teeth of her whose reign is over-past,
But for her stubborn attitude and ineradicable guile.
Stern, sulphurous dogma t'wards the rude she holds, and, with the
  Augur's smile,
Dispenses where strong Doubt is rife (being cloven-tongued and double
  faced)
Her Waters of Eternal Life diluted to the drinker's taste.

Arrogantly she doth persist in claims that crumble at the test
Of Reason, the keen analyst.　Though the well-proved—the trustiest
Pilots of Intellect her ark have left, a floundering derelict ;
Though of authority stripped stark, a spectacle, she stands convict
Of million immoralities, her oracles discredited,
Yet, obstinate, she still denies all light divine but that *she* shed.

We of the wider hope and thought, would she recant, are willing still
To recognise the good she wrought as partly balancing the ill.
But, lo, she is as one that stands upon the main-truck's footing small,

And cannot, though right fain, use hands to clamber down without a
    fall.
For her no more to claim to be sole mouth-piece of the Holy One
Would hasten such catastrophe as needs must leave her clean undone.

But, *till* that day, nor truce nor cess of conflict will there be, nor lack
Of eager-soulèd recruits to press, impetuous, to the attack.
Each morn that dawns, each sun that sets, beholds her enemies' advance,
Beholds enrolment of cadets. Her dupes are wakening from their
    trance ;
No gear but hatred of deceit they need to rout her and compel
Her veterans to make complete surrender of her citadel.

Long as she uttereth the lie of a primeval curse shall we
Assail her and her deity as most *un*holy ; long as she
Across the grave at man doth fling her blasphemous malignities ;
Long as she doth assert a single claim as being more than this—
One evolutionary force, one factor in the growth of good,
That sped our race along its course t'wards universal brotherhood.

Maybe ye ask : *If God ne'er spake direct to Moses on the Mount,
Nor, taking flesh, taught by the Lake of Galilee—if this we count
As fable, dubious is our plight. What certainty—what guarantee
That Right, in human eyes, is Right, that Sin is really Sin, have we?
Whence came the Decalogue, whereto ye yield obedience—from Man?
How, then, are ye assured 'tis true, and part of the Almighty's plan?*

*Setting our sacred creeds aside, if souls must ever be content
To take mere human voice for guide, no surety, but bewilderment,
Must be our wretched state for aye. Though men taught truth before
    our Lord,
They did but stumble on the Way; 'tis now attested by his Word.
On what foundation would ye build, to what firm bed-rock would ye go,
If that prediction were fulfilled which tells our System's overthrow?*

Such words evince that deep disease wherefrom ye must be shaken free—
The soul's desire for slothful ease, its craving for Finality.
Buddha the wise can here instil a truth into the Christian mind :—
"Though many a veil may lift, there will be ever veil on veil behind."
That rock immutable ye seek, nowhere exists for soul or sense ;
Man ever built, and grew from weak to strong, upon Experience.

And what is that whereon *ye* base such servile, blind, unquestioning
    faith—
Is it not this : That in *such* place in Scripture such an one "thus saith"?
The Church of Rome was wise to make her claim.* Of what avail to us
A Voice that long aforetime spake, unless it be continuous ?
Ye hold your Book for true, I wis, because ye are so told ; what then ?
Why, ye have nothing more than this—*faith in the faith of other men.*

We yield in reverence to none, nor chary of due praise are we
For that immortalisēd One—type of divinest charity.
Whether of flesh, in part·or whole, or if but an ideal wrought
And imaged forth from out the soul of sad humanity; though naught
But a sweet-featured myth to whom the quickened conscience of the age
Clung struggling for deliverance from the grossness of Rome's tutelage.

Or man or mythus, we revere that Figure hallowed and enshrined,
Than whose was ne'er more simple, clear, yet blessēd message to man-
    kind ;
We grant its truth as from above, yet hold we what it hath of good
Not *more* of God than is the love, the selflessness of motherhood ;
Than the heart-impulse to adore and deify th' heroic-souled
That moved our ancestors before a song was sung or tale was told.

We hold the spirit breathed therein not *more* divine than was the flame
That glowed in others of our kin whose lives illumed the past ; the same
That tipped the tongue of Cicero, and guided Euclid when he wrought

* Claim to Papal Infallibility.

As pioneer to whom we owe the scaling-steps of highest thought ;
That kindled Curtius* to his leap, Leonidas to bar the pass,
Damon his plighted word to keep, and lit the heart of Pythias.

But think'st thou 'twas th' inherent worth—the dazzling truth of this, thy
    creed,
That moved the princes of the earth to foster it and spread its seed ?
Those crafty savages were keen to see that naught within their ken
Could prove so mighty a machine for making slaves of sturdy men.
They judged aright ; they had the wit to hail and echo its commands,
To urge its precepts, and to fit the gentlest to their iron hands.

Right willing converts did they prove ; what creed more welcome to the
    strong ?
For lo, a voice as from above forbade resistance unto wrong.
They grasped a faith so full of grace and promise as a very jewel—
It taught submission blind and base to tyranny, however cruel ;
It taught endurance dumb, inert, under the burden and the rod :
Slight need the despot to convert ; small marvel 'twas proclaimed of
    God !

The charity ye name of Christ lit not the heart of prince or priest—
To mouth and prate thereof sufficed ; and of the blessèd Three the
    least
Enforced in deed, as though of small avail to save the soul, was *this ;*
But all the parasitic, all the stupefying falsities
Devised by zealotry of old, that stultified the nascent faith,
Were forced upon mankind to hold e'en under penalty of death.

These falsehoods and the priests thereof we gird our loins to assail ;
At these we fling the gibe and scoff, if other speech may not avail.
These, consecrated, championed, borne abroad at point of sword and
    lance,

* The birth, ministry, and crucifixion of Jesus are not one whit better attested,
historically, than is the heroic deed of Curtius. There must have been a certain
divinity in the moral atmosphere to generate the earlier legend.

Though hideous nightmares that the morn shall scatter, yet forbid
    advance.
These spectres, still, on Sabbath days start up across the pilgrim's path,
And shriek aloud in all the ways the gospel of eternal wrath.

The name wherewith ye would attest and stamp these blasphemies hath
    been
The motto of the cruelest and blackest fiends the world hath seen ;
The lip-cry of man's direst foes ; their invocation as they lit
The martyr's pyre and watched his throes : for this we loathe the sound
    of it.
Nay, it but stiffeneth our knees when mouthed by *you* in the same breath
With such profanities as these, for 'tis a very Word of Death.

Was it omniscience to reveal truth of such import as concerned
All humankind's eternal weal, by means and in such wise as turned
The warrior's sword, the zealot's tongue, the student's heart against
    their kin ;
Ne'er to disperse the mists that hung, opaque, around its origin ?
Was't loving mercy so to word such message that it wrought to man
More hurt and misery, and stirred more strife than aught since Time
    began ?

Was it omnipotence to vouchsafe but such ill-guarded testament
As hath been borne to us, a waif upon the flood of accident ;
A transcript torn, defaced ; a scroll not more attested—nay, less well—
Than any glyphic mummy-roll ; one that but few can even spell ;
And one whose garbled fragments set most learnèd doctors by the ears
O'er their decipherment even yet, while reverent Scepticism sneers ?

If thy religion be the true, and doubt thereof be deadliest sin,
Among the bold heresiarchs who found naught of saving grace therein
Whom must ye count ?   Accursèd, lost, and driven from their Father's
    face—

There, 'mid the shrieking holocaust, thy God exacteth ye must place
The gentlest, purest, noblest sons of earth, the selfless and the sage ;
The grandest, the sublimest ones, who wrought for love, nor looked for
    wage.

Writhing, incarcerate, among the flame-tormented there must be
The paladins of Thought, of Song, of Science, of Philosophy,
The fruits of whose life-labour bless uncounted millions of their kind ;
Whose music lightens toil and stress, awakening in the worldliest mind
Echoes in holiest antiphon ; whose work illumes, relieves, and saves
Even the pharisee that on the Sabbath spits upon their graves.

Whom must ye count as surely saved, and set among the seraphim ?
They that with human ashes paved the blackened earth ; they that
    made dim
With tears the eyes—with anguish mad the hearts of millions of their
    kin ;
They that but cursed the world, and bade its children sow no hopes
    therein ;
They that but sorrow wrought, and death ; the cruel, the craven, and
    the foul ;
Each monster that with dying breath but gasped thy creed—and saved
    his soul.

Meseems this gospel-truth hath need of many an apologist ;
How comes it, if 'tis God's indeed ? Betake thee unto church, and list
To the State-hireling hypocrites, who, finding godliness great gain,
Renounce their conscience and their wits. To make th' eternal mystery
    plain,.
Yea into Nay they deftly change—and Nay as deftly into Yea ;
Syntax inspired they re-arrange, and with the words of Scripture play

E'en as a juggler with his balls ; by subtleties tortuous, serpentine,
They prove the infamous and false to be the gracious and divine ;
A message of despair to man—if words hold meaning—they translate

As solace ; everlasting ban as blessing ; and, the while ye wait,
Fables that in our race's youth bemused the barbarous will be
Transmuted into holy truth by theologic alchemy.

The honest souls who truly find glad tidings of great joy in this
We pity, as we do the blind, nor grudge their miserable bliss.
But Falsehood throned ne'er lacks its troop of mercenaries, base as
    bold,
Traitors to Intellect, that stoop to sell their supple tongues for gold ;
Blasphemers of most impious sort, most infidel and mischievous ;
On such, with justice, we retort these epithets they fling at *us*.

No lie too monstrous, and no wrong, for learnēd pundits to maintain
As true and Heaven-ordained, so long as the great multitude remain
Too fearful or too indolent to use their spiritual eyes,
And speak their inmost thought ; content egregiously to subsidise
Self-interest to defend a Faith that filleth with such goodly things
Its hierophants, and halloweth the tyranny of priests and kings.

What spiritual faith soe'er—what dogmas touching things divine—
Could thrive in the same atmosphere, find kindred sustenance, and
    twine
Round the same hearts where grew such foul, pestiferous, and bitter bane
As ripened in the jealous soul of bigot Ferdinand of Spain,
And filled the brains that could devise the Inquisition's devilment—
Of such, all human sense outcries " A lie ! a lie self-evident !"

Whatsoever faith could flourish in the mental soil and air
That could generate and nourish fanatism till it bare
Such horrid fruitage as the work of St. Bartholomew's red night
(When torch and arquebuse and dirk wrought service in the Church's
    sight),
As the cruel work of Calvin's hands—Alva's, the crimes of Benedict
And pious Torquemada, stands at Reason's bar thrice self-convict.

A creed belief wherein can stir to strife—whereof the logic leads
The sanctimonious murderer to perpetrate atrocious deeds ;
A creed that could engender hate so merciless in man that he
Could torture, burn, and mutilate his kin with equanimity
For immaterial mistake in mysteries beyond all ken ;
A faith that, firmly held, can make a hell of earth and fiends of men,

Betokeneth its origin—betrayeth whence it was inspired—
Beareth its condemnation in the curse of those whom most it fired.
Humanity revolts thereat, calm Intellect derides it all,
And Science, silent, long hath sat weaving its winding-sheet and pall.
Time shall demolish and efface that hideous falsity, and bring
To birth a better cultured race, unfrighted by the fatal thing.

      *   *   *   *   *   *

Nay, the evangel ye pretend was sped to earth from Heaven direct
Did never in such wise descend ; therein keen, reverent eyes detect
No revelation breaking through the order that we see around ;
Nor heaven nor earth *proclaims* the True. Your theologic scheme is found
To be of human germ and growth, born of the fertile heart and brain,
And, like all earth-seed, holding both of goodly fruit and deadly bane.

Priestcraft, in league with temporal powers, by arts of pharmacy malign
Extracted from the holiest flowers that round the soul of man did twine—
The very sweetest, fairest plants that in his teeming heart-soil sprang,
Most deadly drugs, intoxicants, like to curare and to bangue,
That paralysed his human-hood and sunk him into stupor dull,
Or maddened him to deeds of blood and infamies unspeakable :

The while, his spiritual lords throve, plundering him bereft of sense,
And, by the murderous dirks and swords of fanatics, gained opulence.
So doth the sovereign of to-day, whose treasury is overfilled,

Draw gold for hoard or vain display from potent poison-drops distilled
From the God-given wholesome grain. Twin foes, these, of the
    commonweal ;
They thrive but by the lack and bane of those they feign to guard and
    heal.

We grant 'twas piety did move patristic zealots to surround
The jewels Charity and Love, that were to them as newly found,
With laboured safeguard of their own—hard masonry cemented fast,
And set them in such altar-stone as, walled and sheltered from the blast
Of stormful times, should aye withstand, even unto the end of days,
The stroke of sacrilegious hand : for this we yield them meed of praise.

A monument of zealous care for holiest things that structure stands ;
But they that built were unaware that Truth, howe'er divine, expands—
That Thought was destined to be free ; and thus their edifice became
A citadel for Tyranny—right glad of sanction to proclaim
Th' immutability of things whereby the fair and fruitful earth
Was but the appanage of kings, to feed their lusts and make them mirth.

The fabric piety designed became the hold of all to whom
The brighter promise for mankind foretold a surer, swifter doom ;
Of all man's foes—the federated despots that foresaw their fall
In each and any change of state that tended to the weal of all ;
Of all the prideful powers that sought to crush, enslave, and render dumb
The peoples, and to stifle thought. But now that fortress hath become

A fortress but in phantasy. For as the trellised creepers hide
Some mouldering ruin from the eye, so through the soil on either side
Pity and Humankindness sprung, a verdant bine whose clustering boughs
With thicket overgrowth have hung the walls of that stern prison-house,
Have interlaced into a mass of densest foliaged evergreen,
High-mantling, so by none that pass can any masonry be seen,

Nor sign of structure anywhere. Part, and peer through that wall of
leaves—
No solid barriers are there !   He who so penetrates perceives
The living tendrils have in-grown and crumbled the cement away
From base to cope ; each loosened stone is honeycombed with such
decay
They are no more than fragile crust, and at the leagued assailants' blow
The whole would topple into dust.   Faith's stronghold now is even so.

Ye who in chorus mouth the words of unintelligible creeds
(With prayers that are but welded sherds of censers found among the
weeds
O'ergrowing pagan altars), say, know ye at all whose work they be ?
Know ye whose mandate ye obey, saying, "Three in One, and One in
Three,"
With other jargon intricate, that neither ye nor any sage,
Howe'er inspired by pious hate, can find upon your sacred page ?

Zealous for holy-days and feasts, none of these things ye know—nor
care ;
But, smiling, pay your unctuous priests to prophesy smooth things and
fair ;
To promise you salvation, though ye play the murderer and thief
E'en to your very death-day, so ye but profess the true Belief—
That thus of sin ye may be quit ; exhorting only that ye strive
To hold *the* Faith, nor fail one whit, and save your wretched souls alive.

As in the days of Constantine, faith subsidised becometh proud.
Th' imperial creed is the divine—for courtiers, for the servile crowd
That ever hasten to avow belief in any patent fraud,
And scramble eagerly to bow to any fetish, and applaud
Whatever mummery it please the Dandy-Royal to make the mode ;
Whose tongues, as supple as their knees, can pæan merge in palinode.

Ye that of Christian England prate, ye smug believers, sleek, serene,
Would ye behold a wondrous great conversion, such as ne'er was seen?
Ye feign to ban the demon Doubt; let but its voice speak from the
    throne—
The million-throated realm would shout the heresy it dares not own.
Ye copy, as ye do the cloth and cut of royalty's pantaloons,
Your Christianity—and both unto your souls are equal boons.

A foolish Faith, a barbarous Creed, at best, are these ye feign to hold.
How long will't be before ye heed this truth, as simple as 'tis old:—
Nor God nor son of God can save the sinner from the doom of sin,
Nor any from the circling wave of consequence to all within
The influence of the evil thing. *This* faith, firm-held, made manifest
In every act, shall surely bring salvation to the sinfullest.

Of this the wise were well-assured a thousand years before your Christ;
Since whom it hath become obscured, the Church declaring it sufficed
To grovel, suppliant, craven-wise, for pardon through another's blood
Shed in vicarious sacrifice—and sanctified such dastard-hood!
Thus wrought she ills the most malign, in that her discipline did draw
Mankind from faith in the Divine Immutability of Law.

The narrow hopes, the selfish aims, the horror of her sacred page
Aglare with Hell's tormenting flames, our stupor 'neath her tutelage,
Are as a nightmare of our youth. Thank God, whate'er—where'er He be,
Who from her paralysing " Truth " hath set our fainting spirits free!
Free to proclaim abroad—aloud the frauds, the infamies she wrought
To hold man's soul enslaved and cowed, and maim the pinions of his
    thought.

Free to approach that Altar High she hath ensanguined and defaced;
To bid our spell-bound brother lie no longer grovelling, self-abased,
In sordid sanctimonious dust, and teach him that his winged career

Is hindered but by self-mistrust, and bounded only by his fear;
That, high or deep, there lieth naught that's needful for the sons of men
Beyond the grasp of human thought, or out of range of mortal ken.

The storm that shall disperse the blight of falsity and fear she cast
Approacheth; to our hopeful sight the scud thereof is flying past;
Men's souls, like buds in arid land, are all athirst, and pray 'twere here
To freshen, so they might expand.   'Twas long a-brew, and in *her* ear
It rumbleth but as yet afar; so sniffs she high, and in her pride
Still thinks to stay the dawn, to bar the sunshine, and arrest the tide,—

Aye, the dawn of a to-morrow when the righteous shall prevail,
And the bloodshed and the sorrow she hath wrought be as a tale;
The sunshine of great gladness in deliverance from her creed
That drove men into madness, being set before the deed;
The tide that shall o'erleap her when it riseth in the day
Of the tempest that shall sweep her and her blasphemies away!

CHAPTER AND VERSE

FOR STATEMENTS MADE OR IMPLIED IN THE FOREGOING.

With acknowledgments, for material, to the Writings of MRS. ANNIE BESANT,
JULIAN, MR. BRADLAUGH, SALADIN, MR. G. W. FOOTE, *and Others.*

THE object of this Appendix is to assist the young investigator to a
knowledge of certain important facts, especially of Church history,
which are studiously veiled or ignored in the ordinary books of instruc-
tion, and are admitted by tutors only with extreme reluctance. The
reason of this concealment must be that the truth is in reality some-
thing very different from, or even the exact opposite of, what is
generally taught.

"A plotter of high treason to the people "—*p. 16.*
See any English History, reign of James I., for account of that
monarch's disputes with the House of Commons; and the sturdy oppo-
sition to his pretensions maintained by his second and last Parliaments.
See, also, how all the principal offices of State were filled by the
creatures of Buckingham, who ruled the king as he pleased.
Sophia, the grand-daughter of James I., having married the Duke of
Brunswick, was the ancestress of the present reigning family of Guelphs.

" One whose right to rule derives through yet another's tainted blood "—*p. 16.*

As the right to the crown was transmitted, through the "tainted blood" of James II., to Queen Anne, the failure of whose issue brought the House of Brunswick to the throne of England, it may be said of Victoria that her "right to rule derives" through James II., the grandson of James I. That such a creature as James II. should have been held as transmitting the sacred right of sovereignty to his offspring is the fact the writer wishes to emphasize for consideration.

" Genius hath the record graven of that doubly treacherous one "—*p. 16.*

See Macaulay's portrait of James II., done in indelible ink.

" A scion called to reign, yet half afraid to cross the seas
To guard his faithful people's weal "—*p. 16.*

See Thackeray's " Four Georges " and Hallam's " History."

" Bemired the fount of honour......
So that the taint became contagious even to the best "—*p. 17.*

The Triennial Parliaments were lengthened by a corrupt majority. For the committal of the Septennial Bill there was a majority of seventy-two ; and about eighty-two members of the House had either fingered Walpole's gold or pocketed the bank-notes left "by accident" under their plates.

In the ten years which preceded the Septennial Act the sum expended for Secret Service was £337,960. In the ten years following the passing of that Act the sum expended for Secret Service was £1,453,400.

See records of the reign of George I.

" Mark ye that alien race ; with one tradition are they all imbued "—*p. 17.*

It was gravely maintained (by the Stuarts and their adherents) that the Supreme Being regarded hereditary monarchy, as opposed to other forms of government, with peculiar favour ; that the rule of succession, in order of primogeniture, was a divine institution, anterior to the Christian, and even to the Mosaic, dispensation ; that no human power could deprive the legitimate prince of his " rights ;" that his authority was necessarily always despotic ; that the laws by which, in England and other countries, the prerogative was limited were to be regarded merely as concessions which the sovereign had freely made, and might at his pleasure resume; and that any treaty into which a king might enter with his people was merely a declaration of his present intentions, and not a contract of which the performance could be demanded (Macaulay).

Anyone whose duties have brought him within the circle of the Court of Victoria, and into personal contact with the chief members of the Guelph Family, must have discerned the scarce-concealed resentment they feel at the constitutional restraints imposed on them. They are arrant Stuarts in temperament and disposition, with the Hanoverian miserliness and stolidity superadded. They by no means heartily accept their position, exalted and luxurious though it be; and even the careless observer " in close attendance " can see their mental attitude to be that of injured divinities, chafing under a wrongful deprivation of much of their due freedom, splendour, and prerogative by a pestilent democratic spirit. (G. H. M.'s note; compared with, and abundantly corroborated by, those of others who have had the same opportunities of observing as himself.)

> " The care that chiefly stirreth these royal dullards to activity
> Is to make safe and hide the keys of their vast wealth from scrutiny "—*p. 18.*

In no single matter did Queen Victoria display such great and anxious activity as in that of preventing the publication of the Prince Consort's will, which has never been proved.

> " Brunswick's swarm of harpies "—*p. 18.*

George I. brought with him no wife to England, but he was accompanied by at least two of his mistresses; and our peerage roll was enriched by the addition of Madame Kilmansegg as Countess of Darlington, and Mademoiselle Erangard Melosine de Schulenberg as Duchess of Kendal and Munster, Baroness of Glastonbury and Countess of Faversham.

Lord Chesterfield says of George I.: "No woman came amiss to him, if she were only very willing and very fat."

John Heneage Jesse, in his " Memoirs of the Court of England," speaking of the Duchess of Kendal, the Countess of Platen (George I.'s co-partner in the murder of Philip, Count Konigsmark), and others less known to infamy, says: "George I. had the folly and wickedness to encumber himself with a seraglio of German prostitutes." The Duchess of Kendal had £7,500 a year, the profits of the place of Master of the Horse, and much other plunder from the national purse.

" To grasp and to retain, but nought bestow "—*p. 18.*

During the present reign only, the Royal Family has obtained from the nation *twenty-four million pounds*, while 1,225,000 people have died of starvation in Ireland alone.

Queen Victoria's first message to Parliament was a request for provision for her mother, and her last a request for provision for her granddaughter.

Her numerous progeny are all kept by the nation ; for Her Majesty, though fabulously rich—indeed, " rich beyond the dreams of avarice " —is too mean to maintain her own children. The *people* support them, and in most extravagant idleness ; they never did anything, and never expect to do anything ; they are the recipients of public charity, which does not change its essence because administered by special Acts of Parliament (G. W. Foote's " Royal Paupers ").

" Mark the hybrid Church that flung its shadow o'er the people's homes "—*p. 21.*

Neal, in his " History of the Puritans," vol. i., p. 28, says : "*Reign of Henry VIII.*—There was a very odd execution .of Protestants and Papists at the same time. Three Protestants, all clergymen and Lutherans, were sent to the Tower for offensive sermons..........Four Papists were, by the same Act, attainted for denying the King's supremacy. The Protestants were burned and the Papists hanged." Thus bloodily was founded the Church established by law. See also Lord Herbert of Cherbury's account of the cruel enforcement of the Statute of the Six Articles.

" No pretence can be more opposed to the facts of history than the pretence that the Reformation was the work of the Church of England reforming itself. Had Henry VIII. obtained the Pope's sanction to his divorce from Catherine, he would never have rejected the Papal supremacy ; but he found the Romish Church standing in his path to Anne Boleyn, so he struck it down and cast it out of his way. One of the earliest acts of the new Church was to legalise Henry's union with Anne, and it as readily divorced her, when Henry was weary of her, as it had divorced Catherine. It proved itself ever willing to pander to that monarch's lust or hate, and has ever since been an abject and contemptible creature of the Crown." (See Mrs. Besant's " Sins of the Church of England.")

" Thus free were the peoples, till that day when there appeared in Eastern lands,
Girt with spears and armed array, a Symbol borne by bloody hands "—*p. 21.*

" The policy of the emperors and senate, as far as it concerned religion, was happily seconded by the reflections of the enlightened, and by the habits of the superstitious, part of their subjects. The various modes of worship which prevailed in the Roman world were all considered by the people as equally true, by the philosopher as equally false, and by the magistrate as equally useful. And thus toleration produced not only mutual indulgence, but even religious concord " (Gibbon, " Decline and Fall," chap. ii., sec. 1).

" Constantine had a father-in-law (Maximian) whom he impelled to hang himself; a brother-in-law (Licinius) whom he ordered to be strangled ; a nephew, about twelve years old (Cæsar Licinius), whose throat he ordered to be cut ; an eldest son (Crispus) whom he beheaded ; and a wife (Fausta) whom he had suffocated in a hot bath " (Voltaire).

" He (Constantine) pursued the great object of his ambition through the dark and bloody paths of war and policy ; and, after the victory, he abandoned himself, without moderation, to the abuse of his fortune......
As he gradually advanced in the knowledge of [Christian] truth, he proportionably declined in the practice of virtue ; and the same year of his reign in which he convened the Council of Nice was polluted by the......murder of his eldest son " (Gibbon, " Decline and Fall," chap. xx.).

" Ever, since the Fathers fooled him, since the pontiffs held their sway "—*p. 25.*

B. H. Cowper, a champion of Christianity, in his " Introduction to the Apocrypha," p. 25, says, speaking of the Early Fathers : " Ancient invention and industry even produced sundry scraps about Herod, Veronica, Lentulus, and Abgar, wrote epistles for Christ and his mother, and I know not how much besides. No difficulty stood in the way ; ancient documents could easily be appealed to *without necessarily existing ;* spirits could be summoned from the other world by a stroke of the pen, and be made to say anything ; and sacred names could be made the passport to fictions *ad libitum.*"

Pope Boniface VIII. (1295–1303) had his predecessor, Celestine, put in prison, where he died. He styled himself King of Kings ; he trafficked in Indulgences, and declared all excluded from Heaven who disputed his claim to universal dominion. He persecuted the Ghibellines, and ordered the city of Prieneste to be entirely destroyed. He was publicly accused of simony, assassination, usury, of living in concubinage with his two nieces, of having children by them, and of using the money received for indulgences to pay the Saracens for invading Italy.

See " Frauds and Follies of the Fathers," by J. M. Wheeler, and Ranke's " Lives of the Popes."

" Ever hath she striven to mar the dawning smile of Liberty "—*p. 27.*

Pope Gregory XVI., in an encyclical letter, dated August, 1832, says: " It is from that most fetid fountain, Indifferentism, springs the absurd and mistaken notion that Liberty of Conscience is to be recognised and vindicated. What has prepared the way for this most pestilent error is, that ample and immoderate Liberty of Opinion which is spreading far and wide, to the ruin of Church and State.........This is the aim of that worst of all liberties, that never-enough-to-be-execrated and detestable Liberty of the Press *(huc spectat deterrima illa ac nunquam satis execranda et detestabilis libertas artis librariæ ad scripta quælibet edenda in vulgus)*" (John Robertson, Coupar Angus).

Study, also, the votings of the English bench of Bishops against every measure for relieving or enlightening the people, down to the last extension of the franchise.

" Bear your witness, O ye martyrs done to death—but not o'erawed,
Were not her Decretal charters forgeries and based on fraud ?"—*p 29.*

For an account of the forgeries known as the Decretal Epistles and the Donation to Constantine (described by Gibbon as the two magic pillars of the spiritual and temporal monarchy of the popes) see Gibbon's " Decline and Fall," chap. xlix., sec. 2 ; " Chambers's Encyclopædia," article " Canon Law ;" Mosheim in his section on the ninth century ; and Robertson's " History of the Christian Church."

" Are but dully acquiescent where our sires were protestant "—*p. 30.*

The orthodox upholder of the authority of the Bible, loud in praise of the Reformers who fought for *that* as the sole basis of their faith, quite overlooks the fact that *they* honestly and sincerely *believed* in the complete harmony of Reason and the Bible ; *they* had no doubts whatever to smother concerning the entire agreement of the two. But could they revive, with our fuller knowledge, and be called upon to decide the question as now presented to us, to settle the new difficulties which cause such frantic and pitiable attempts at reconciling the patent absurdities of Scripture with the latest discoveries of Science, who can doubt that they would to-day be among the champions of Freethought and Reason, as against Scriptural authority ?

" She (whom truly nothing shameth), having done her best and worst
To retard and damn it, claimeth to have blessed it from the first !"—*p. 30.*

Note the *volte-face* executed by the Christian Church with regard to the question of Slavery, both in the West Indies and the United States.

Note the bitter opposition made, especially by the Scotch clergy, to the introduction of the use of anæsthetics.

Note the Church's opposition to the Education Acts.

Compare her attitude towards Charles Darwin, on the first appearance of his "Origin of Species," with her half-hearted, surreptitious adoption of his theory on its endorsement by the scientific sense of Europe; and behold her—hear her now, precisely in the spirit of the patristic forgers and interpolaters, doing bare-faced and flagrant violence to the "Holy" text in order to square it with the doctrine of Evolution.

Note the gymnastic efforts of Mr. Gladstone, in his "Proem to Genesis" (most probably written at the request of a deputation of distressed bishops), to prove that the so-called Mosaic account of Creation accurately pre-figures the cosmic plan now, after long research, proved to be the true one. Observe the sublime and eminently Christian arrogance with which he relegates the noble discoverers in astronomy and geology to the position of mere journeymen, who but fill in the details of the vast panorama limned in grand, but perfectly *correct*, outline by that inspired artist, the author of the Book of Genesis !

" We know thy Church but thieved these gems and set them as her own "—*p. 33.*

Translation of the text of Confucius B.C. *500 (Josephus Tela's edition, 1691), Maxim 24.*	*Text of St. Matthew (whoever he may have been) vi. 12.*
Do to another what you would he should do unto you ; and do not unto another what you would not should be done to you. Thou only needest this law alone; it is the foundation and principle of all the rest.	Therefore all things whatsoever ye would that men should do unto you, do ye even so unto them ; for this is the law and the prophets.

Confucius, on being asked, "What do you say concerning the principle that injury should be repaid with kindness?" replied : "With what, then, will ye repay kindness ? Nay, recompense injury with *justice*, and kindness with kindness."

There was no sane, practical maxim taught by Christ that had not been enjoined by such teachers as Thales, Solon, Pythagoras, Confucius, Plato, Socrates, the Brahmins, the Peripatetics, the Therapeuts, and the Stoics.

See Moncure D. Conway's "Sacred Anthology" for numerous other instances of moral maxims, old and long current before the time of Jesus, and now incorporated among his supposed sayings.

"Thy Gospel, by whose hands 'twas writ thou knowest no more than any child "
—*p. 35.*

Faustus, Bishop of Riez, A.D. 472–490, declared it to be "certain that
the New Testament was not written by Christ nor by any of his Apostles,
but a long while after them by some unknown persons who, lest they
should not be credited when they wrote of affairs they were little
acquainted with, affixed to their works the names of Apostles, or of such
as were supposed to have been their companions" (see Lardner's
"Credibility," vol. ii., p. 221).

It is still uncertain when, in what language, and by whom the Four
Gospels were written. Probably not one of the gospels, as now known,
existed in the first century; and the Fourth Gospel could not have
existed in the lifetime of Papias, who died A.D. 164. Jesus and his
apostles must have spoken a corrupt Hebrew tongue, called Syro-
Chaldee ; and it is maintained by learned authorities that the Greek
text of the New Testament is a translation from Latin MSS. No
original MS. of any one of the gospels is extant, the oldest being pre-
sumably of the fourth or fifth century. These facts do not detract from
any intrinsic merits the gospels possess ; but they do very seriously
affect the credit of the Church that represents these books to be con-
temporary documents by eye-witnesses of the events related therein.

"The Council praying for a sign "—*p. 35.*

In A.D. 325 was held the first Council of Nice, under the presidency
of Constantine. At this Council a definite creed was first formulated
and declared necessary for salvation.

At this Council, says Pappus in his "Synodicon" (written at about
that period), the Canon of Scripture was determined.

"'Twas not till after centuries three that any book thereof was held
As of supreme authority "—*p. 35.*

Dr. Lardner says : "The canon of the New Testament had not
been settled by any authority that was decisive and universally acknowledged, but people judged for themselves as to the genuineness of
writings proposed to them as apostolical, even so late as the time of
Cassiodorus, A.D. 526."

"And many a zealous scribe did add thereto whate'er he deemed they lacked "—*p. 35.*

Mosheim says, in "Ecclesiastical History," vol. i., pp. 358, 359 :
"The greatest and most pious teachers of the fourth century were
nearly all infected with this leprosy" (of fraud). He alludes to the

"base audacity of those who did not blush to palm their own spurious productions on the great men of former times, and even on Christ himself and his apostles, so that they might be able, in councils and in their books, to oppose names against names and authorities against authorities. The whole Christian Church was in this century over-whelmed with these disgraceful fictions."

No period in the history of the world ever produced so many spurious works as the *first two or three* centuries of our era. No fable could be too gross, no invention too transparent, for men's unsuspicious acceptance, if it assumed a pious form. The name of every apostle or Christian teacher, not excepting that of the great Master himself, was freely attached to every sort of religious forgery.

See Bishop Ellicott's "Cambridge Essays for 1856," pp. 175, 176; and Gibbon's "Decline and Fall," chap. xv., p. 207.

We know from Origen, A D. 250, that Celsus, an Epicurean philosopher, who wrote A.D. 160, complained that the Christians were perpetually altering and correcting their gospels.

See, further, "Chambers's Encyclopædia," where, under the article "Bible," the keen and careful reader will find admissions of such great uncertainty as to the authorship and date of production of the various books of the New Testament, as render it impossible for any mind (except the theological) to reconcile them with the idea of a Revelation of the highest importance direct from God, the reception of which is absolutely necessary to the salvation of every human being.

See also the Preface to the recently-issued Revised Version of the Bible. In that Preface the impartial reader will discern, through the sonorous euphemisms and sanctimonious vapourings of the authors, a real and direct charge of dishonest translation against previous translators; and an admission that the revisers themselves are extremely doubtful as to whether they have succeeded in rendering God's meaning as He intended. How does this square with the Sixth Article of the Church? and how does it harmonise with her tone towards her Sunday-school pupils, and that of her missionaries towards the heathen?

> " The tome she quotes
> As Holy Writ was but declared the word of God by human votes "—*p. 35.*

The Council of Laodicea, held in A.D. 366, excluded (by vote) the apocryphal writings from the canonical Scriptures; but, in A.D. 397, the Council of Carthage declared (by vote) those writings to be of equal value with the rest of the Bible. The Church of Rome sides with the Council of Carthage, the Church of England with that of Laodicea.

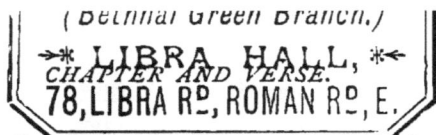

Which of these two Councils was guided unto all truth by the Holy
Ghost ? The English Church, to be consistent, must hold the bishops
composing the latter Council to have been miraculously and infallibly
inspired equally with the writers of the Gospels. But logic and theology
are irreconcilable opponents.

"Did mystic Paul when he rebelled ?"—*p. 36.*

Against the Church of Jerusalem, at the head of which was James
(the brother of the Lord) ; which was composed of the actual hearers
and authorised expounders of the teachings of Jesus ; and which was
established before there was time for his words to fade from their
memory, or to be modified by novel doctrines (I am assuming the truth
of the Church's own tradition). To that Church, of James and Peter,
Paul was in sharp and direct opposition ; nor were the two parties ever
really reconciled. The efforts of our Doctors of Divinity to heal or
hide that breach are vastly entertaining. (See Francis W. Newman's
"Against Hero-Making in Religion.")

" Whose authoritative voice cried, ' Quibblers, cease !' "—*p. 36.*

See Gibbon, ibid, chap. xxi., p. 321, paragraph "Indifference of
Constantine."

" How tigerish was their hateful strife "—*p. 36.*

See Gibbon, ibid, the whole of chaps. xxi. and xlvii.

" Thy creed, that after centuries seven
A half-barbaric Frankish king approved as final and of Heaven "—*p. 36.*

At Verden, in A.D. 782, Charlemagne caused 4,500 Saxon prisoners
to be massacred in cold blood (White's " Elements of History ").

Gibbon, in his " Decline and Fall," chap. xlix., sec. 2, speaking of
Charlemagne, says : " Of his moral virtues chastity is not the most con-
spicuous ; but the public happiness could not be materially injured by
his nine wives......the various indulgence of meaner or more transient
amours, the multitude of his bastards whom he bestowed on the Church,
and the long celibacy and licentious manners of his daughters, whom
the father was suspected of loving with too fond a passion."

Among the severities of Charlemagne was his institution of the
Secret Tribunal of Westphalia, a sort of inquisition appointed to punish
the heresy of the Saxons. This terrible system lasted till 1650, when
the elector, Frederick William, shocked at its enormities, effected its
abolition (White's " Elements ").

Charlemagne died A.D. 814.

In A.D. 809 the Council of Aix-la-Chapelle condemned the Greek Church of damnable heresy. What was this deadly sin of the Greek Church? Simply this: it refused to give credit to a forgery introduced surreptitiously into the creed by Recared, King of the Spanish Visigoths, at the Council of Toledo in 589. At that Council the Western Church had wanted to prove the Trinity, so it had slyly foisted into the creed the duplex word, "filio-que" (and the Son): "I believe in the Holy Ghost proceeding from the Father [filio-que—and the Son]." "We will not have it," said the Greek Church; "it is not in the bond." "You *must* have it," said the Western Church; "and, if it is not in the creed, it ought to be there." "We wont have it," said the Greeks. "You *shall* have it," said the Romans. And the two Churches have been cat and dog ever since.

Charlemagne made a law that anyone who rejected the words from the creed "*salvus esse non potest.*" The Council of Toledo had said "Filio-que;" the Council of Aix-la-Chapelle said "Filio-que;" Recared and Charlemagne voted for "Filio-que." The Greek Church cried "No filio-que;" Pope Leo III. cried "No filio-que;" and ancient creeds up to A.D. 589 had declared "No filio-que." Three against four; so the "filio-ques" carried it; and "filio-que" it is up to the present day in the Latin and English creed.

The Holy Ghost "proceeds from the Father and the Son" because a Gothic King of Spain had the audacity to make the interpolation, and Charlemagne had the arm of strength to insist that whoever would not accept the forgery could not be saved! This is the way our doctrines have been made for us. (See Julian's "Pillars of the Church," Appendix.)

"Thus through the Church's whole career bloodguiltiness and guile are seen"
—*p. 37.*

In nothing has the Church been so consistent as in the implacability and meanness of her methods towards those who either silently ignore her pretensions, or oppose them with the weapons of reason. Since Hypatia—gashed and hacked to death piecemeal, under the shadow of the crucifix, by a Christian mob instigated by a Christian patriarch—down to the latest preacher deprived of his benefice, her mode of answering the arguments of doubters has been the same in spirit as that of Cyril of Alexandria. The power only, not the will, has been lacking in these later days; for the modern equivalents of the rack and stake are her last recourse against unanswerable objectors.

The method adopted by the saintly Fathers of the fourth century against Porphyry affords an instance of peculiarly despicable malignity. "Porphyry, a Platonist (A.D. 233–305), acquired the surname of the Virtuous ; and he brought such formidable objections and such unanswerable arguments against the Christian legend that all his real writings were burnt by the order of the Christian Emperor Theodosius, A.D. 388 ;" and only such fragments of his writings as Christians themselves had "controverted" and garbled, or as, torn from their context, stood as orthodox admissions, were permitted to come down to us.

This is an illustration of the early Christian manner of conducting theological debate.

"Whether (Christ was) of flesh in part or whole —— "—*p. 39.*

The facts cited below go far to justify the impartial truthseeker in doubting whether the Jesus of the Gospels is a strictly historical character.

We do not possess the unimpeachable testimony of a single writer known with certainty to have been an eye-witness of Jesus. A mass of manufactured testimony relating to him, purporting to be that of his contemporaries, has at last been abandoned as wholly fictitious, though zealous Christians still present it as genuine where they know they are safe from contradiction. Paul—an impracticable mystic and egotist, the perfect prototype of a Salvation Army captain—never saw Jesus, and disdained everything in the way of evidence concerning him.

The epistles attributed to James and Jude, 2 Peter, and 2 and 3 John are of most doubtful authorship ; some of them speak of matters of ecclesiastical polity which had no establishment or existence until long after the first century ; and the Apocalypse has been accepted and rejected by Council after Council.

1 Peter and 1 John, the least disputed of the writings of supposed companions of Jesus (but which may easily have been altered and "corrected" by later hands), contain only some vague allusions which might be construed as those of eye-witnesses of his sufferings.

The authorship of the writings attributed to Barnabas, Hermas, Clement of Rome, Ignatius, and Polycarp is matter of great dispute ; but, whoever the authors were, they display an egregious readiness to believe and assert, on the merest hearsay, miracles the most monstrous, grotesque, and futile ; and their writings, in their entirety, are most inconvenient witnesses for "the Truth." Of the four so-called evangelists it is sufficient to say that divines are driven to the most laboured efforts, the most strained interpretations—amounting even to absolute misreading of Scripture, and to the wildest guessing, in order to fix the identity of Matthew, Mark, Luke, and John with any person named in the Bible.

Such is the untrustworthy, dubious, and even shadowy character of the witnesses who attest the events of the life of Jesus.

Now as to perfectly independent testimony :

The nearest contemporaries of Jesus whose writings we have are Seneca, who was about twenty years old at the supposed date of the Crucifixion ; the elder Pliny, who was about ten years old at that period, and lived to the age of fifty-six ; Philo, who lived from B.C. 20 to A.D. 45 ; and Josephus, who lived from A.D. 37 to 93.

Neither Seneca, Pliny, nor Philo makes the least allusion to Jesus ; though the first two made a particular study of everything in the way of the marvellous. (See Gibbon's remarks on this in " Decline and Fall," chap. xv.)

In Josephus occurs a passage ("Antiquities," bk. xviii., chap. iii.) mentioning "Jesus called Christ." This passage was *first* quoted by Eusebius—on whose testimony all Ante-Nicene ecclesiastical history practically depends—who exults over it as a prodigious prize, his exultation itself serving to awaken suspicion that it was another of his own audacious forgeries. (For his capabilities in that line see Lardner's "Credibility.")

The passage is now universally admitted to have been interpolated between the time of Origen, A.D. 230, *and that of Eusebius*, A.D. 316 (see Gibbon's " Decline and Fall," chap. xvi., p. 214, footnote).

But one other allusion occurs—viz., "to James, the brother of Jesus " ("Antiquities," bk. xx., chap. ix.). But, as this has not been so persistently flourished in the face of the sceptic by Christian evidence-mongers, we may well suspect a passage which *they* are chary of adducing.

It is a patent fact that the world contains no record of any other character whose existence as a real personage was denied, and even disclaimed, as soon as ever it was asserted, as was the case with Jesus. See in Lardner's " Credibility" the number and variety of " heresies " current in the first and second centuries—a period commonly represented by the clergy to their ignorant hearers as an age of sweet concord of belief and harmonious piety among Christians.

It is also undeniable that the year and even the place of the birth of Jesus are *unknown ;* that the length of his ministry and the date of his execution are equally uncertain to the student of history ; that the name of Jesus was as common among the Jews as the name of Smith is with us ; that the word "Christos," signifying "the anointed," is given to all the Kings of Judah and Israel, and to other potentates

—such as Cyrus, King of Persia, but the translators have studiously rendered it as Christ *only* in relation to Jesus ; and that the nearer we get to that period, the more do we find diversity of opinion as to whether Jesus was a man or a myth, and the more extravagant and grotesque are the stories of him and his doings. We also find Irenæus, A.D. 177, declaring that the ministry of Jesus extended over ten years, and that Jesus lived to be fifty years of age ("Against Heresies," bk. ii., chap. xxii.).

The ordinary Christian, densely ignorant of the history of his own faith, is unaware that the 25th of December was an ancient pagan festival. The zodiacal sign of the Virgin then shows on the eastern horizon, the sun is one degree above the solstitial point, and the year is new-born. Thus, on that day, were born (of virgin mothers) all the sun-gods of antiquity. The Latin Church, in the second half of the fourth century, fixed that day as the birthday of Christ : and by such arbitrary fiat has a baseless priestly fiction survived as a historical fact through twenty generations of unthinking believers.

The legends of Jupiter, of Bacchus, of Æsculapius, of Horus, of Ching-mou, and of certain Babylonian deities, present collectively every miraculous incident related of the birth, life, death, and resurrection of Jesus. The legends of Osiris and of Chrishna are each startlingly similar, even in minute details, to the Christian story. And to Horus were applied the titles, Good Shepherd, Lamb of God, Bread of Life, the Door of Life, the Fan-bearer, and the Truth. The characteristically arrogant assumption of Christian writers, that the Chrishna legend was borrowed from their gospel, has been demonstrated to be as false as most other "Christian evidences" prove to be on critical examination. (See J. M. Robertson's "Christ and Krishna.")

"The paladins of Thought, of Song, of Science, of Philosophy "—*p. 42.*

Jeremy Bentham	La Place	Schiller
Lord Bolingbroke	Gibbon	George Eliot
Giordano Bruno	Goethe	Harriet Martineau
Denis Diderot	Grote	George Sand
David Hume	R. W. Emerson	Charles Dickens
Humboldt	Thomas Carlyle	Henry Hetherington
Victor Hugo	Heinrich Heine	Robert Burns
Charles Darwin	Garibaldi	Shakespeare
John Stuart Mill	Shelley	Spinoza
Robert Owen	Longfellow	Benjamin Franklin

The mighty minds, the large and tender hearts of these, were never confined by the narrow creeds and articles of the Christian Church ; the spirit breathed in the writings even of those whom she impudently claims as believers (Shakespeare, Burns, and Dickens) gives the lie direct to her central dogmas, and is daily working their dissolution. At the bare mention of the names of Voltaire and Thomas Paine fashionable orthodoxy shudders with horror, without ever having read a single line of their writings, or having acquainted itself with a single detail of their lives, except the fact that they believed in an infinitely more just and merciful deity than Jehovah.   The ostracism of these two noble names from polite conversation among Christians is another instance of the mental servitude of the " respectable " classes to an unscrupulous clergy.

Two more utterly selfless, generous champions of liberty and humanity never lived than Voltaire and Paine : throughout their lives they fought valiantly against every form of tyranny, cruelty, and super-stition ; and, as a consequence, the placeman and the priest have foully aspersed their characters, pursuing their memories with the most despic-able and malicious falsehoods.

"The while, his spiritual lords throve, plundering him bereft of sense "—*p. 44.*

See Jortin, vol. iii., p. 228, concerning the "millennial craze ": " It was one of those frivolous and senseless notions which the priests in-dustriously cherished for the sake of lucre."   " At the close of the tenth century it was believed that the end of the world was approaching, the clergy having assiduously prepared men's minds for the expectation. Hence it came to pass that an innumerable multitude, leaving their possessions, and giving them to churches and monasteries, repaired to Palestine, where they were told that Christ would descend from Heaven to judge the world.   Others solemnly devoted all their goods to churches and to the clergy, and entered into their service as bond-slaves, performing a daily task."

See also Ranke's " Lives of the Popes."

" Ye who in chorus mouth the words of unintelligible creeds
(With prayers that are but welded sherds of censers found among the weeds
O'ergrowing pagan altars) —— "—*p. 46.*

The Nicene Creed was first formulated at Nicæa at the Council held there A.D. 325.

The Apostles' Creed was first received into the Latin Church, in its present form, in the eleventh century ; but some parts of it were formu-lated in the fourth and fifth centuries.

The Athanasian Creed was received into the Western Church in 670. Not until the reign of Charlemagne was the doctrine of the Trinity asserted and enforced with the minute and emphatic delineation it presents in the Prayer Book.

See Gibbon's "Decline and Fall," chap. xxi., for account of the Arian controversy through the reigns of Constantine and his sons. He says, in an aside: "As those princes presumed to extend their despotism over the faith as well as over the lives of their subjects, the weight of their suffrage sometimes inclined the ecclesiastical balance; and the prerogatives of the King of Heaven were settled or changed or modified in the cabinet of an earthly monarch."

Christianity conquered Paganism, but Paganism infected Christianity. The rites of the Pantheon passed into her worship, and the subtleties of the Academy into her creed (Macaulay).

And, to conclude, in the words of the learned Bunsen: "It should long ago have been acknowledged that our present popular and school chronology is a fable strung together by ignorance and fraud, and persisted in out of superstition and intellectual lethargy."